CINCO THE CLINIC CAT
Cinco, el gato de la clínica

Carol Brickell

Illustrated by Jim Hastings

Spanish Translation by Lali Miles

BROWN BOOKS KIDS

Cinco the Clinic Cat
Cinco, el gato de la clínica

Brown Books Kids
Dallas / New York
www.BrownBooksKids.com
(972) 381-0009

A New Era in Publishing®

Publisher's Cataloging-In-Publication Data

Names: Brickell, Carol, author. | Hastings, Jim, illustrator. | Miles, Lali, translator.
Title: Cinco the clinic cat = Cinco, el gato de la clínica / Carol Brickell ; illustrated by Jim Hastings ; Spanish translation by Lali Miles.
Other Titles: Cinco, el gato de la clínica
Description: [Second edition]. | Dallas ; New York : Brown Books Kids, [an imprint of] Brown Books Publishing Group, [2021] | Bilingual. Parallel text in English and Spanish on the same page. | Interest age level: 004-012. | Summary: "When school is out, Alisa spends each day with her sister, who works in a medical clinic. But Alisa feels alone and out of place. One day, she sees a new face--a stray cat. After five days, they become friends and she names him Cinco. Together, they get involved in the activities at the medical clinic--and make more friends along the way"--Provided by publisher.
Identifiers: ISBN 9781612545363
Subjects: LCSH: Cats--Juvenile fiction. | Sisters--Juvenile fiction. | Clinics--Juvenile fiction. | Friendship--Juvenile fiction. | Honduras--Juvenile fiction. | CYAC: Cats--Fiction. | Sisters--Fiction. | Clinics--Fiction. | Friendship--Fiction. | Honduras--Fiction. | Spanish language materials--Bilingual.
Classification: LCC PZ7.B7591 Ci 2021 | DDC [E]--dc23

ISBN 978-1-61254-536-3
LCCN 2021908348

Printed in China
10 9 8 7 6 5 4 3 2 1

For more information or to contact the author, please go to
CincoTheClinicCat.com.

Acknowledgments

This book is dedicated to the people that I have met in Honduras who have shown warm hospitality and friendship as we have worked together.

I'd like to thank the amazing group of people that I travel with each year to Honduras. I'd also like to thank the staff at Brown Books Publishing Group for their support of this project.

A special thanks goes to María de la Paz Del Cioppo, Juan Vertiz Melchor, and Nora Acevedo for their valuable assistance with the translation.

Proceeds from the sale of this book will go to charities that support medical clinics and provide medical supplies to those in need in Latin America.

Agradecimientos

***E**ste libro está dedicado a la gente que he conocido en Honduras, que me ha demostrado la hospitalidad y la amistad mientras hemos trabajado juntos.*

Me gustaría dar las gracias al grupo de gente increíble que me acompaña a Honduras cada año. También le agradezco al personal de Brown Books Publishing Group por su apoyo a este proyecto.

Un agradecimiento especial le doy a María de la Paz Del Cioppo, a Juan Vertiz Melchor y a Nora Acevedo por su valiosa ayuda con la traducción.

El producto de la venta de este libro irá a organizaciones de beneficencia que apoyan clínicas médicas y proporcionan suministros médicos a los necesitados en América Latina.

Foreword

I am honored to write the foreword to Carol Brickell's award-winning children's book, *Cinco the Clinic Cat*. I have known Carol for many years and had the opportunity to sign her daughter's well-used copy of *The 7 Habits of Highly Effective Teens*. Her love and compassion for humanity shine through in this heartfelt children's book, as well as in her broader mission to help those in need around the world. Not surprisingly, this unique book has received two awards: the Moonbeam Children's Book Award and the Mom's Choice Gold Award.

As you read *Cinco the Clinic Cat*, you'll be reminded that life is better when you can make a friend along the way and make a difference in the lives of others. The story is based on actual service work at a clinic in Honduras. Carol served with a group of volunteers who did eye tests and distributed donated eyeglasses. *Cinco the Clinic Cat*'s beautiful illustrations depict scenes that were painted from actual photographs of the clinic and the clinic cat.

One of the reasons I love this book is because it aligns with my philosophy that life is a mission and not a career. A career asks, "What's in it for me?" A mission asks, "How can I make a difference?" When Carol does book readings, young people are often led to ask, "How can I make a difference?"

As the author of *The 7 Habits of Highly Effective Teens*, I applaud Carol for her commitment to teaching our youth about the value of volunteering to help others and for donating a portion of the proceeds to clinics in need in Latin America.

Cinco the Clinic Cat teaches children the value of friendship and the importance of serving others while they are also exposed to another language in this bilingual book. This book has something for everyone, young and old!

—Sean Covey
President of FranklinCovey Education
New York Times Best-Selling Author of
The 7 Habits of Happy Kids and
The 7 Habits of Highly Effective Teens

Prólogo

*E*s un honor para mí escribir el prólogo del premiado libro infantil de Carol Brickell, Cinco, el Gato de la Clínica. *Conozco a Carol desde hace muchos años y tuve la oportunidad de autografiar la copia bien utilizada de su hija de 7 Hábitos de los Adolescentes Altamente Efectivos. Su amor y compasión por la humanidad brillan en este sincero libro para niños, así como en su misión de ayudar a los necesitados del mundo. No es sorprendente que este libro único haya recibido dos premios: el premio al libro infantil* Moonbeam *y el premio* Mom's Choice Gold.

Al leer Cinco, el Gato de la Clínica, *se le recordará que la vida es mejor cuando puede hacer un amigo en el camino y marcar la diferencia en la vida de los demás. La historia se basa en el trabajo de servicio real en una clínica en Honduras. Carol sirvió con un grupo de voluntarios que hicieron exámenes oculares y distribuyeron anteojos donados. Las hermosas ilustraciones de* Cinco, el Gato de la Clínica *representan escenas que fueron pintadas a partir de fotografías reales de la clínica y el gato de la clínica.*

Una de las razones por las que amo este libro es porque se alinea con mi filosofía de que la vida es una misión y no una carrera. Una carrera pregunta: "¿Qué gano yo?" Una misión pregunta: "¿Cómo puedo marcar la diferencia?" Cuando Carol hace lecturas de libros, los jóvenes a menudo se preguntan: "¿Cómo puedo hacer una diferencia?"

Como el autor de 7 Hábitos de los Adolescentes Altamente Efectivos, aplaudo el compromiso de Carol de enseñar a nuestros jóvenes sobre el valor del voluntariado para ayudar a otros y de donar una parte de las ganancias a clínicas necesitadas en América Latina.

El libro Cinco, el Gato de la Clínica *les enseña a los niños el valor de la amistad y la importancia de servir a los demás mientras también están expuestos a otro idioma en este libro bilingüe. ¡Este libro tiene algo para todos, jóvenes y mayores!*

—*Sean Covey*
Presidente de FranklinCovey Education
Autor mas vendido del New York Times
7 Hábitos de los Niños Felices *y*
7 Hábitos de los Adolescentes Altamente Efectivos

"I wonder if my wish will come true."

"Me pregunto si mi deseo se hará realidad."

Alisa lives in a country called Honduras. When there is no school, Alisa goes with her sister Karen to a clinic in their neighborhood. "I'd like to help Karen, but I only get in the way. I wish I had a friend."

Alisa vive en un país llamado Honduras. Cuando no hay escuela, Alisa va con su hermana Karen a una clínica en su barrio. "Quisiera ayudar a Karen, pero me resulta difícil. Me gustaría tener un amigo."

That day, Alisa sees a new face.

Ese día, Alisa ve una cara nueva.

On the second day, she sees the cat again. "Kitty, are you hungry?"

Al segundo día, ella ve al gato de nuevo. "Gatito, ¿tienes hambre?"

On the third day, Alisa feeds him again. "Do you need a friend? I can be your friend."

Al tercer día, Alisa le da de comer de nuevo. "¿Necesitas un amigo? Yo puedo ser tu amigo."

On the fourth day, he returns. "Maybe you'll stay this time."

Al cuarto día, vuelve el gato. "Tal vez te quedarás esta vez."

On the fifth day, he stays. "We became friends in five days. I'll call you Cinco."

Al quinto día, se queda el gato. "Nos hicimos amigos en cinco días. Te llamaré Cinco."

"Karen, look! Everybody likes Cinco. Can he stay at the clinic?"

"¡Karen, mira! A todo el mundo le gusta Cinco. ¿Puede quedarse en la clínica?"

Karen smiles. "Yes, he's welcome at the clinic. He makes the patients happy. Why don't you and Cinco play with the children who are waiting?"

Karen sonríe. "Sí, es bienvenido en la clínica. Él hace feliz a los pacientes. ¿Por qué no juegan ustedes con los niños que están esperando?"

"There's Marcos from my school.   He looks sad."

"Ahí está Marcos de mi escuela. Él se ve triste."

"You may have to wait a long time," Alisa says to Marcos. "Come play soccer with us."

Marcos shakes his head.

"*Puede ser que tengas que esperar mucho tiempo,*" *dice Alisa a Marcos.* "*Ven a jugar al fútbol con nosotros.*"

Marcos niega con la cabeza.

"Marcos needs glasses. He can't see the blackboard at school."

"*Marcos necesita anteojos. No puede ver la pizarra en la escuela.*"

"Bring Marcos back next week," Karen says. "My friends are coming. They will bring eyeglasses and other medical supplies."

"Tráelo a Marcos la semana que viene," dice Karen. "Mis amigos están llegando. Ellos traerán anteojos y otras provisiones médicas."

Alisa and Cinco keep watch for Karen's friends to arrive. "Look Cinco! They're here!"

Alisa y Cinco esperan la llegada de los amigos de Karen. "¡Mira Cinco! ¡Ellos están aquí!"

"Cinco, that's people medicine!"

"*¡Cinco! ¡La medicina para la gente!*"

Karen gives Marcos an eye test to find out how well he can see.
"Can you read the top letter?"

Karen realiza un examen de la vista a Marcos y revisa si puede ver bien.
"¿Puedes leer la letra de arriba?"

"We don't have the right glasses," Karen says. "We'll try to make you some."

"No tenemos los anteojos necesarios," dice Karen. "Vamos a tratar de hacer unos especiales."

"Marcos, I hope they can make glasses that will fit you," Alisa says.

"*Marcos, espero que puedan hacer unos anteojos que te sirvan,*" *dice Alisa.*

"Cinco, I see you now! I thought you were a little dog."

"*¡Cinco, te veo ahora! Pensé que eras un perrito.*"

"Tonight, we will have a party in honor of our friends!" Karen says.

"¡Esta noche, tendremos una fiesta en honor a nuestros amigos!" dice Karen.

"Thank you for being our friends. Here is some special pottery that we make here in Honduras."

"*Gracias por ser nuestros amigos. Esta es una cerámica especial que hacemos aquí en Honduras.*"

"I like playing soccer now that I can see the ball!"

"¡Me gusta jugar al fútbol ahora que puedo ver la pelota!"

"Goodbye, Marcos. We'll have fun when school begins."

"Adiós, Marcos. Nos divertiremos cuando empiece la escuela."

"Cinco, my wish came true the day I met you."

"Cinco, mi deseo se hizo realidad el día que te conocí."

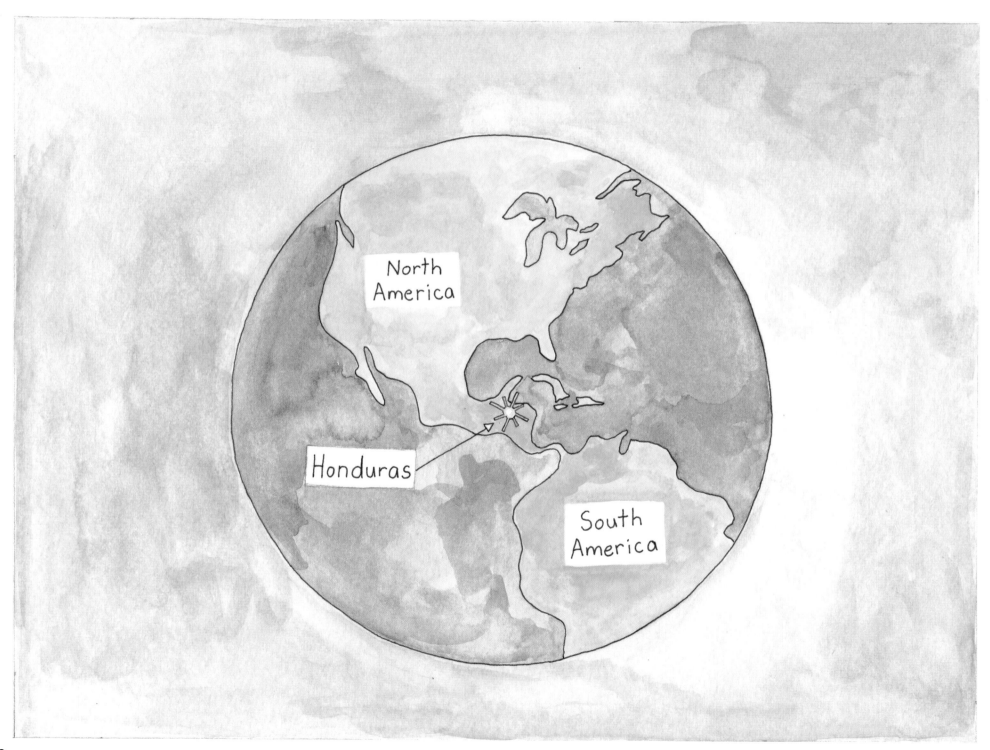

CINCO THE CLINIC CAT
Cinco, el gato de la clínica

There is a beautiful place in Central America with high mountains, tropical forests, brightly colored birds, and warm, sandy beaches. In this country named Honduras, many people work in the fields and grow some of the bananas and pineapples that you see in grocery stores.

Hay un hermoso lugar en Centroamérica, con altas montañas, bosques tropicales, pájaros de colores brillantes y lindas playas de arena. En este país llamado Honduras, mucha gente trabaja en los campos y cultiva algunos de los plátanos y las piñas que se venden en los supermercados.

About the Author

Carol Brickell lives and works in Dallas, Texas. She loves to travel once a year to work in a school and clinic in Honduras. When visiting the school and clinic, she enjoys singing songs with children, reading stories, and giving eye tests. She is married, has two grown daughters, and has two cats she adopted from a local pet orphanage.

About the Illustrator

Jim Hastings also lives and works in Dallas, Texas. He is an elementary school art teacher, as well as a drawing and painting instructor at Studio Arts Dallas. Jim earned a BFA from the Kansas City Art Institute and an MA in Art Education from the University of North Texas. He is married with five children. As a young artist, cats were one of Jim's favorite subjects. More than likely this interest in cats came from watching the exploits of Miss Kitty, a tabby who slept at Jim's feet for years.